MW01492505

Software for the Soul

Psalms for Everyone

Discovering the Inner meanings

Software for the Soul

Psalms for Everyone -

Discovering the Inner Meanings

Tara Mizrachi

Foreward by Rabbi Moshe Feller

Edited by Mrs. Mendele Feller Z"L

Copyright © 2012 by Tara Mizrachi
All rights reserved

ISBN-13: 978-1515378211
ISBN-10: 1515378217

Library of Congress Catalog Number:
Call #   BS1440 .M58 2012x

Unless otherwise noted, the English translations of Psalms are
reproduced with kind permission from:

"Tehillim Ohel Yosef Yitzchak with English Translation"
© 2012 (5773)
Kehot Publication Society,
770 Eastern Parkway, Brooklyn, New York 11213

Free Downloadable Content
Gam Ki Elech, Lev Tahor, Hodu, Keli Ata & Pitchu Li recorded
with kind permission from:

Tara Publications
29 Derby Ave., Cedarhurst,, NY 11516

בס"ד

With abundant gratitude to Hashem:

In loving memory of:

SALLY FUCHS *(z"l)*

&

MORRIS MIZRACHI *(z"l)*

Dedicated to my children: Estee Mae, Judy, Sarah and Mark Moshe; and to my husband Victor and to my teacher Rebbetzin Chayale Gourarie.

5

CHABAD LUBAVITCH

UPPER MIDWEST MERKOS

Rabbi Moshe Feller
•Director

Rabbi Gershon Grossbaum
•Director of Development

Rabbi Manis Friedman
•Dean, Bais Chana

Mrs. Hinda Leah Sharfstein
•Director, Bais Chana

Rabbi Shlomo Bendet
•Director, Lubavitch Cheder Day School

Rabbi Yisroel Goldberg
•Principal, Lubavitch Cheder Day School

Rabbi Mordechai Friedman
•Lubavitch Cheder, instructor

Rabbi Menachem Mendel Feller
•Chabad Lubavitch of West S. Paul

Rabbi Mordechai Grossbaum
•The Living Legacy
•Chabad Lubavitch of Minneapolis

Rabbi Yosef Skagalow
•Chabad Lubavitch Minyon of S. Louis Park

Rabbi Dovid Greene
•Chabad Lubavitch of Southern MN-Rochester

Rabbi Zalman Bendet
•Chabad Lubavitch of Greater St. Paul

Rabbi Yonah Grossman
•Chabad Lubavitch of Fargo, North Dakota

Rabbi Nachman Wilhelm
•Dean, Lubavitch Online Smicha

Rabbi Yitzi and Chavi Steiner
•Chabad, University of Minnesota

Rabbi Moshe Kasowitz
•Inward Bound

Rabbi Yosaif Grossbaum
Mrs. Naomi Grossbaum
•Gan Israel Day Camp
•Onog Shabbas V'Yom Tov

Rabbi Mayer Rubiafeld
•Special Projects Coordinator

Rabbi Levi Y. Feller
Rabbi Yonah Goldberg
•Chaplaincy Service

Chabad Lubavitch – Upper Midwest Merkos
1748 Hampshire Court, S. Paul, MN 55116
651.698.3858 fax 651-698-1295 lubavitchmn@aol.com

By the Grace of G-d
5 Menachem Av 5774
Yahrtzeit of the Ari-Zal
Aug. 1, 14

SOFTWARE FOR THE SOUL
PSALMS FOR EVERYONE

Dovid Hamelech and all the authors of the book of Tehillim owe Tara Mizrachi a debt of gratitude for her very scholarly and deeply inspiring treatise on Tehillim, SOFTWARE FOR THE SOUL -- PSALMS FOR EVERYONE. She has indeed made the book of Psalms relevant for everyone. Her style of highlighting what Tehillim has to say about every aspect of life and all of life's situations is refreshing and very insightful.

Tara, this was a work waiting to be written, and G-d gave you the merit of doing so.

May "Software for the Soul" evoke for you and your family G-d's blessings for long life, good health, and success in all your endeavors. Be assured that "Software for the Soul" will hasten the coming of Moshiach.

With Esteem and Blessing,

Contents

Foreward by
Rabbi Moshe Feller

By the Grace of G-d
5 Menachem Av 5774
Yahrzeit of the Ari-Zal
Aug. 1, 14

SOFTWARE FOR THE SOUL – PSALMS FOR EVERYONE

Dovid Hamelech and all the authors of the Book of Tehillim owe Tara Mizrachi a debt of gratitude for her very scholarly and deeply inspiring treatise on Tehillim.
SOFTWARE FOR THE SOUL-PSALMS FOR EVERYONE.

She has indeed made the Book of Psalms relevant for everyone. Her style of highlighting what Tehillim has to say about every aspect of life and all of life's situations is refreshing and very insightful.

Tara, this was a work waiting to be written and G-d gave you the merit of doing so.

May Software for the Soul evoke for you and your family G-d's blessings for long life, good health and success in all your endeavors. Be assured that "Software for the Soul" will hasten the coming of the Moshiach.

With Esteem and Blessing,

Moshe Feller
Director Upper Midwest Merkos
Chabad Lubavitch

Introduction

.

If you are reading this introduction, you likely have an interest in The Book of Psalms which in Hebrew is called "Tehillim," meaning "Praises."

Maybe you read psalms occasionally but the meaning escapes you, and you want to learn more about the psalms, as they were written in the language of origin.

Maybe you never read from the Book of Psalms, but you're interested in the words which have inspired so many for thousands of years.

Maybe you read Psalms every day, but after reading the same passages so many times, the depth of the inspiration you once felt has diminished over time. You may be looking for an extra insight, an extra glimpse into the beyond so that the depth of feelings and understanding as you are praying to God, ("kevanah" in Hebrew) is increased.

Why Recite the Psalms?

"If we knew the power of the verses of Psalms
and their effect in the celestial heights,
we would recite them constantly.
Know that the chapters of Psalms break through all barriers
and soar aloft from level to level unimpeded.
They intercede before the Master of the Universe
and secure their effect with kindness and mercy." –
"The Tzemach Tzedek",

3rd Lubavitcher Rebbe, (1789-1866)

Reciting Psalms is a way that each of us can make the world a better place. Jewish people and people of many faiths, from all walks of life, in all parts of the world, for thousands of years have prayed songs of Psalms during times of joy, sadness and every day events.

Once I was in Israel walking to the Kotel, the Western Wall. Alongside me was the joyful sight and sound of high school girls walking quickly on their way to pray. Suddenly, the announcement blared on the loudspeaker: A suspicious package had been found. As we waited for the bag to be safely exploded by the soldiers, I noticed many of the girls began to calmly read from the Book of Psalms. After a while I asked one of the girls which chapter of Psalms she was reading since a bag containing a bomb was just found that may have been planned with these young school girls in mind. I was curious to know if there was a special psalm one reads in a situation such as this: "avoiding a bomb about to explode," "surviving a close call," perhaps? She smiled softly: "Oh yes, Thursday's chapter." It became evident that every day is a miracle. Every day is a reason to recite Psalms.

One day, I was riding in a bus traveling to Safed, a day before the yahrzeit of Rabbi Shimon Bar Yochai. The bus filled up with passengers and it became apparent that there were too many passengers and not enough seats. The young men stood allowing older passengers to be seated; then they sat on the floor of the bus. After the bus traveled for a short while, a woman opened a box containing the 150 chapters of Tehillim (Psalms) in individual paper pamphlets. She began passing them out, and before I knew it, we were no longer a bus of random strangers. We were now a bus filled with people with a purpose: Each of us doing our part to bring increased holiness into the world, to make the world a more positive place. During that bus ride one entire Book of Psalms was recited. When we reached our destination, there were expressions of contentment on many of the faces of the people stepping off the bus. In a way, it is analogous to our life on earth. Reciting Tehillim can bring holiness. It is something each of us can do, wherever our journey takes us.

According to Jewish teachings, psalms are like a special telephone with a direct line that connects you with the Creator of the World. You make connections with those who have recited psalms throughout history, connections with those your prayers are helping and connections with the Creator of the World.

By reciting psalms, each of us, regardless of where we live, can contribute in our own unique way and increase the holiness of the world. Taken cumulatively, these positive actions can go a long way to tipping the balance and lead the world to a better tomorrow.

Each of us can help the world one Psalm at a time.

A Solitary Flame

It was but a moment of eternity that the earth stood still and a solitary flame shone as if in defiance. A flame whose life, it seemed, would surely blink out with little more than a whisper. Miriam was lighting the Shabbas candles.

Deborah shifted her tired feet quietly, so as not to disturb her friend. But it would not be easy to distract Miriam this moment, for in her heart a miracle was taking place. The chances of her Shabbas candle flickering out, not reaching for the sun, were as unlikely as the chances of her soul not reaching for its eternal source.

Deborah watched the ceremony. For some reason it seemed vaguely familiar. "Such an interesting sounding language..." she gazed out the window in thought.

Deborah noticed the Azalea flowers of violet and pink which peaked from beneath the window. She saw the date trees in the distance which held promise of sweetness in the midst of this harsh landscape. She smelled the delicate fragrance of buttercup flowers, near the door, which blended with the sweet aroma of apples, cinnamon and freshly baked challah.

Miriam finished reciting the blessings on the candles. She turned to her friend and smiled warmly.

"Good Shabbas, Deborah," she said.

Deborah's eyes sparkled with gratitude. Miriam had acquired much knowledge over the course of her lifetime and her personality exuded a loving and accepting quality.

Deborah looked around and scanned the room. Beyond the kitchen table, books of varying sizes graced the bookshelves that covered two walls of Miriam's small kitchen. Deborah's eyes narrowed as she focused to read the words. Some of the books had Hebrew inscriptions on their bindings. She thought about the Torah that was also written in this holy language. Miriam had once told her that God created the entire universe using the letters of the Hebrew alphabet, and that King David and the other Jewish sages of Israel wrote in Hebrew.

She noticed the variety of reading material. Next to the Farmer's Almanac on the third shelf were books on physics and astronomy with scribbled yellow "post it" notes appearing from within their pages. Of all the books on her shelves, however, there was one special book which was most often in Miriam's hands.

After they ate and talked for a while, Deborah reached over to the book shelf and touched the special brown book with Hebrew and English letters etched on the cover.

"Miriam, I always see you reading this book," she said. "Please tell me all about it." Deborah was fascinated and wanted to know all about this special book.

"It is the Book of Psalms. It is called the 'Tehillim' which means "praises" in Hebrew," Miriam explained. "The element of the

17

miraculous is ever present in the Book of Psalms. Of all the books of the Torah, it is the one book in which a person is communicating with God. The Five Books of Moses, the Prophets and the Book of Writings depict events in which God is communicating with man. After God created the entire universe, foretold to Abraham a future which didn't seem possible, and freed the Hebrew slaves giving to them insights far beyond their time, it is appropriate to respond in awe and appreciation for the miracles He created and continues to create for us. This is the purpose of Psalms.

"Thus, it is fitting that the words of the psalms have been sung, danced and expressed with love and hope for more than 3,000 years. "Women and men, young and old, people of all faiths and all varieties of religious expression have prayed from their Book of Psalms during times of need. People gather in groups and recite the entire Book of Psalms to bring increased holiness into the world and to give extra strength to those who are ill. Some people, like me, just read a little every day.

"The Book of Psalms is 'Software for the Soul.' It offers each person a user friendly way to give praise and gratitude for the One who creates all and who grants love and compassion, comfort and strength.

18

"Were psalms recited long ago?" "How did people experience the psalms during that time?" asked Deborah.

Miriam replied, "In ancient Israel during three major festivals: Passover, Shavuot and Sukkot, the Children of Israel gathered together at the Temple in Jerusalem. They traveled for many miles and over many days. Modern archeologists have discovered routes which contain mikvahs, or sacred springs, along these ancient walking paths which span for many miles in all directions, all leading to Jerusalem.

"As the families walked this long journey, they sang Tehillim or Psalms in praise of the One who has created the world and is the Source of All Blessing. They walked and sang, bringing tambourines, drums and harps along with them. When they camped for the night along the way, they would play their instruments, dance and sing these psalms of praise.

"As the Children of Israel reached Jerusalem, during the Festival of Sukkot, one could see Sukkot or temporary dwelling places for as far as the eye could see. The oil lamps from within these thousands of Sukkot would brighten the night sky.

"The Levites were the tribe assigned by God not to dwell in a particular portion of land but rather to bring music from the heavenly spheres. They were the choir and the orchestra and they practiced for years for these special days. As the people gathered in the Temple, the space was miraculously expanded so that there was room for everyone. And as the Levites ascended the steps of the Temple in Jerusalem they would sing Psalms of Ascent, or Shir Ha Ma'a lot, in Hebrew. These are the same psalms 120 through 134 that we read in this very book.

"Who wrote the psalms?" Deborah asked.

"King David wrote most of the psalms. Asaph, the sons of Korah, Heman, Solomon, Moses, Ethan the Ezrahite and even Adam are all authors of psalms.

"David's melodies gave comfort to King Saul when the king was not feeling well. The psalms touch the soul in infinite ways – bringing comfort, healing and strength to those who are struggling.

"King David faced a wide variety of trials during his lifetime. Since these many experiences are expressed in songs of praise or psalms, it is said there is a psalm to help with just about any question or challenge a person may experience."

Deborah marveled. Questions flowed out and filled the air as effortlessly as the mellifluous chimes and stringed instruments of King David's psalms.

"What does the Book of Psalms say about living each day?"

Miriam glanced at her book. The corners of its brown leather cover were worn to a tattered beige. Peach pie, coffee, and other evidence of life's morsels had left their mark on the pages of her Tehillim book – and especially on the pages Miriam read most often. Phrases were underlined. Penciled notes graced its margins with thoughts like so many Calanit flowers blossoming and withering through the years.

She lovingly turned to the page that revealed a psalm that would answer the young woman's question. She didn't look at the pages however. For Miriam had long ago memorized these passages – these words of comfort, healing and wisdom that connected her like a strong golden path to the people and places long ago and far away who have recited these very same words.

She began to sing a beautiful melody as she recited the words of Psalm 34:13

"Who is the man who desires life?

Loves days to see good?"

(translation by tm)

"Mi ha ish hafetz chaim?

Ohev yamim lirot tov"

Miriam paused. With a wisdom that seemed to carry the peacefulness of the melodies of her Book of Psalms, she began to speak.

"What does it mean to 'love days'?

"In the midst of a challenging occurrence we may remember the day vividly. When we think it may be our last, or when our life is on the brink, that one day becomes all the more precious. What if we were to 'love' our days whether they be 'good' days or 'bad' days or 'ordinary' days?

"From God's perspective every day is precious. If we take on that viewpoint and love each day, accept each day as a loving gift from God, give of our best effort from the moment we awaken to the moment we fall asleep - the Psalmist reveals 'to see good' will surely result."

What does the Book of Psalms say about prayer?

Miriam turned the page to Psalm 118:19 and the melody of the psalm poured forth.

"Open for me the Gates of Righteousness!

I will enter them and praise God"

"Pitchu li sha'arey tzedek…"

"'Pitchu Li' 'Open for me' is not a command but a statement of fact, she said. The Gates are open for me that I may walk through them. They are not fences, walls or bars. They are gates. Unlocked, ready, welcoming and now it is up to me to walk through them.

"How do I walk through them? I open the gates by giving thanks to the Creator of the World. Even when things are not going the way I would like. Even when it seems the world's forces are waged against me. The Psalmist reveals that 'the gates of tsedek, of righteousness, are open to me.' 'I will enter and thank God' - for the blessings that I wished for and for those I would rather have avoided at the time. All are part of God's beautiful and complex symphony of life."

What do Psalms say of kindness?

Miriam sang the words of Psalm 89:3.

"For I have said,

"the world is built with kindness;

there in the heavens

you establish Your faithfulness."

"Olam chesed Yibaneh"

"'The world is built with kindness,' she said.
What does it mean to be 'built' rather than 'created' or 'made'?

'Bara' is written in the Torah when God '<u>cre*ates*</u>' heavens and earth. It says 'Bereishis bara Elokim et ha shamayim v'et ha'aretz' '*Oseh*' is written when God '*makes*' peace in the heavens ('Oseh shalom bimromav'). But in Tehillim 89, Ethan the Ezrahite sings: 'The world is <u>built</u> with kindness' ('Olam chesed yibaneh').

"The word 'built' suggests the world of kindness on earth is not created by a single utterance rather it is built like one builds a house - brick by brick, good deed by good deed, prayer by prayer. The way a world of kindness happens is painstaking and deliberate. It requires many hands and much effort and love - even when we tire and feel like quitting.

"To build a world of Godliness requires each of us, one by one, to live our life in the fullest way possible. The brick of our life may be the corner brick or part of the support beam. We may not be at the top of the highest point but our brick is no less important.

"When God sought to build the world it came from His loving kindness. This teaches us that no matter how impossible things are to understand, whether it is a great personal struggle or a tragic world event, we know God builds a world which manifests His loving kindness for each of us - and each of us assists Him daily in the great task of building his home."

What does the Book of Psalms say about protection?

She turned to the page containing Psalm 31:4

"For you are my rock and my fortress;"

Miriam asked, "What does it mean to be a rock and a fortress?

"A rock does not change with the passing breeze like the wind or the water. It has been with us through the ages. Yet stones placed together form a fortress. There is protection. There is more strength than each has alone.

"If we apply this to our lives, being placed together doesn't mean we must be exactly the same as our neighbor and worship in exactly the same way - for rocks are each unique, but it is important not to struggle against each other, we are asked to hold each other up and respect each other's strengths and weaknesses.

"When we have faith in the unchanging loving kindness of the One who created and sustains the world and when we support and hold each other up, we come to experience that God is indeed our rock and our fortress, timeless through the ages, shielding us from the dangers of uncertain times."

What do Psalms say of speech?

Miriam paused in thought and opened the page to Psalm 19.

"The heavens <u>recount</u>

the glory of the Almighty;

The sky <u>proclaims</u> His handiwork.

Day to day <u>speech</u> streams forth;

Night to night <u>expresses</u> knowledge.

There is no <u>utterance</u>, there are no <u>words</u>;

Their <u>voice</u> is inaudible.

Their arc extends throughout the world;

Their <u>message</u> to the end of the earth"

"Speech is considered a uniquely human attribute. Only man has the complex muscles and nerves, the fine motor skills, necessary to articulate the variety of consonants and vowels that make up human speech. Only man has the mind capable of abstract thought of subjects such as philosophy and mathematics and the need to share ideas, aspirations and even humor.

"While speech may be uniquely human through the instrument of lungs, larynx, tongue, teeth and lips - there is another language that speaks volumes: The heavens, the separation of the waters above and below, the day and the night, the precision of the universe and all that is in it - declare without sound but in the most articulate and clear way. And when we listen carefully the universe speaks directly to our soul.

"When we think about our everyday life, we may look to the heavens for inspiration. For as the beauty and magnificence that is all around us speaks of awesomeness, we are reminded to be kind and loving in our speech as well. In so doing we may, in our unique, special way, emulate the timeless and infinite loving kindness of God's wondrous creation."

What do Psalms say about silence?

She quietly said the words of "Psalm 65:2

"To You, Silence (quiet waiting)

is prayer,

God, in Zion."

(translation by tm)

"Lecha dumia tehilla Elokim b'Zion"

"The most eloquent statements we can say are often without words: The heartfelt connection of a hug, the kindness of a gift. Although we are often full of words, the truest feelings are often expressed nonverbally," she described.

"Since God's attributes are infinite, any attempt to praise Him with words could imply that His attributes are finite and able to

33

be understood, according to Rashi. Therefore, quiet contemplation is the most eloquent praise of God.

"According to the Lachmei Todah, the psalm could also be read correctly as: "Your silence is your praise." referring to God's patience and quietude in his compassion for us.

"When comforting someone, often the best way is not by saying brilliant words but rather being a good listener. Slowing down and patiently listening. Listening is often the best way to show we care.

"With silence, our senses convey the sights, sounds, scents - the windows to our world without which we would be disconnected. Our way of connecting with people and connecting with God is made so much clearer. When we truly listen we can reach a higher awareness of the wisdom of the universe. We can perceive the beautiful world we live in. And then it may be possible to convey these perceptions through loving thoughtful words and actions that speak volumes."

What does the Book of Psalms say of trust?

Miriam sang the words of Psalm 52:10

"I trust in God's kindness

forever and ever"

"Batachti b' chesed Hashem

olam va ed'"

"What does it mean to trust?" she asked.

Miriam paused in thought then said: "A bird trusts that when it holds apart its wings, the wind will carry it above the rooftops and into the sky above. The flower trusts that when it opens its petals water will miraculously quench its thirst.

"The Children of Israel trust when they walk waist deep into the Red Sea, while women lead them with tambourines and songs of

35

joy, somehow the swords and chariots of the great armies of Egypt will not hinder their journey to the land promised by God Himself.

"And you and I trust when we hold open the pages of our blessed Torah, miraculously our thirst will be quenched for then our soul may soar. And like the Children of Israel when we walk waist deep into the dangers of the world, that we will sing songs of faith and love.

"This is very difficult to do, however.
The Psalmist offers some help in maintaining our 'trust' - for the word in this Psalm is 'I trusted' which means 'I trusted.' This reveals that trust is sometimes temporarily forgotten or lost but always present deep inside.

"When we look at our immediate situation however - the flower about to show that it's petals are only paper thin, the bird as it leaps off a rooftop, the Children of Israel when the chariots and swords of the armies are within sight, it is often difficult to trust.

"Yet, when we think of the long road our soul has traveled and has yet to travel, when we remember how our soul trusted then as it trusts now deep inside, it may then be possible to reconnect with the trust in God's kindness that is forever."

What do Psalms say about wisdom?

Miriam opened her book to Psalm 72

"For Solomon:

Elokim Your judgment to the king give;

And your righteousness

to the son of the king."

(translation by tm)

L'Shlomo:

Elokim mishpateycha l'melech ten"

"This is the last of the psalms by David, she explains. As he passes the yolk of leadership to his son, Solomon, he gives his son a blessing that the wisdom to judge be guided by God's infinite wisdom.

"With this, Solomon, whose name is derived from the same root as "peace," does reign. His kingship over Israel is notable for breaking all barriers. Great kindness toward the needy, and with that wealth beyond measure, the building of a Temple so beautiful, it was known far and wide. Its treasure and the Temple's greatness were so vast that when conquered the marble and gold was used to build the Colosseum - the "jewel of Rome" and later quarried to build the Vatican. Its foundation stones were larger and heavier than the stones of the pyramids.

"For King David, the sweet Psalmist of Israel, through whom the timeless praises of God flowed - the most meaningful blessing he could give his son was the blessing of wisdom. And with the blessing of wisdom, all the many blessings of the time of Solomon's reign flowed.

"Wisdom is a quality each of us is able to attain. The eternal wisdom of God is accessible to us since all wisdom ultimately comes from God, the source of all blessing. And so the last psalm of David ends thus:

"Blessed (the source of all blessing)

is the Lord God,

the God of Israel,

who alone performs wonders.

Blessed is His glorious name for ever,

And may the whole earth be filled

with His glory,

Amen, and Amen.

The prayers of David,

son of Jesse are concluded"

What do Psalms say of having faith in the midst of hardship?

Miriam slowly turned the page to psalm 22:2.

She looked up to the heavens and sang a lament of centuries past.

"My God, my God,

Why have you forsaken me!

So far from saving me,"

"Eli, Eli, lama azav tani?"

"The Oral Torah states that King David wrote this Psalm in foreknowledge of the time of Hadassah, also known as Queen Esther.

"Miriam began to tell a story that is recited during the holiday of Purim. It took place at a time during which the Persian Empire ruled the known world beginning in 369 BCE. Persia is located where modern day Iran is today. King Ahasuerus was the

41

military leader and absolute monarch who controlled an empire encompassing 127 provinces.

"As recorded in the Book of Esther, King Ahasuerus held a celebration for 6 months and at one point asked his wife Vashti to appear wearing only her crown so that everyone might admire her beauty. Vashti refused because she was infected with a skin condition. When she refused to appear she was vanquished and the king sought to replace her. He held a beauty contest and chose a young woman named Hadassah who had hidden her Jewish identity and called herself Esther. The chief minister of the empire, a man named Haman, due to a personal hatred, convinced the King to issue a decree that would wipe out all Jews throughout the empire on the 14th of Adar.

"When Queen Esther learned of the plot, she called for three days of fasting and prayer. She then appeared before the king without being summoned, which could have brought upon her the death sentence. She disclosed her identity as a Jewess and appealed to the king to spare the lives of her people. King Ahasuerus allowed the Jews to defend themselves and, in this way, the Jewish people were able to survive.

"One could imagine the despair a person living at that time may have experienced after reading the king's edict. It ordered that the unarmed population consisting of every Jewish man, women and child living in all 127 provinces of the Persian Empire was to be slaughtered."

"The forces in the world of material existence were insurmountable. There seemed to be no place to turn."

"So the Jews reached beyond the physical. They prayed loudly and softly, in groups and solely, wearing sack cloths and fasting, people of all backgrounds and ages bound together in their pureness of faith and prayed. Miraculously, the edict was revoked and the Jewish people survived.

"All this took place over the course of many years. Many non-miraculous but ordinary events occurred that resulted in this great miracle.

"When one looks back and 'all the dots are connected' one can look deeply into these everyday events and realize that just like Hadassah, the seemingly ordinary events of our lives are not ordinary after all.

"When looked at from a distance, over time, the events of our lives may have a purpose that often is not apparent to us while we are in the midst of hardship.

"There may be times in our life when we share the feelings of the psalmists as he cries out: 'My God why have you forsaken me?' But then, we may remember the story of a young woman who helped bring about a miracle of survival. This miracle revealed, although it seemed hopeless by outward appearances, God had not forsaken His children after all.

What does the Book of Psalms say of success?

Miriam turned to Psalm 75:7

"For not from the East or the West,

nor from the desert

does greatness come.

For God is Judge."

"Ki lo mi motsa

u'mi ma'arav

V'lo mi midbar harim

"Ki Elokim shofet."

"If I live my life with the awareness that:
God is the source of my blessing
and not myself;

And God is the true judge, the One I answer to,
and not other people;

Then my life will be filled with humility, courage, contentment
and truth."

What does the Book of Psalms say about God's dwelling places?

Miriam turned to Psalm 84:2

"How beloved are Your dwellings,

O Lord of Hosts!"

"Ma yedidot mishkenoteycha

Hashem Tsevaot"

"The term "God of Hosts" refers to God's sovereignty over all the worlds, spiritual and physical - everywhere and all that is" she said.

"The sons of Korach wrote this Tehillim declaring that God's dwelling places are beloved. This was written after the Temple in "Jerusalem had been destroyed. After witnessing the devastation, memories etched into their minds, emotions and thoughts must have been overwhelming.

"At this moment, they witnessed a bird making its nest. In the midst of the Temple's ruins when it seemed all had been destroyed, Hashem's loving kindness is sovereign over all - and His 'dwelling places' are truly beloved."

What does the Book of Psalms say about the Torah?

She opened the page to Psalm 19:8

"The Torah of Hashem is perfect,

restoring the soul;

The testimony of Hashem is trustworthy,

making wise the simple..."

(translation by tm)

"The first seven sentences of Psalm 19 correspond to the 7 days of creation, she said. Passage 8 describes beautiful things about the Torah. This teaches that when we want to reach higher, we reach for the Torah. When we wish to elevate our spiritual awareness we reach for the Torah.

"Yet when we celebrate the receiving of the Torah at Mount Sinai, rather than go into meditative seclusion, we celebrate by sharing a festive dairy meal with friends and family. We stay up all night and discuss the Book of Ruth and the Ten Commandments.

"Thus, the Torah teaches us about our mission on this earth - not merely to enlighten ourselves spiritually in solitude, but to bring the physical in - to bring holiness into all aspects of life, spiritual and physical."

What does the Book of Psalms say about God's protection?

Miriam opened the book to Psalm 121, raised her eyes heavenward and began:

> *"I lift my eyes to the mountains*
>
> *from where will my help come?*
>
> *My help will come from the Lord,*
>
> *maker of heaven and earth.*
>
> *He will not let your feet falter;*
>
> *your guardian does not slumber.*
>
> *Indeed the Guardian of Israel*
>
> *neither slumbers nor sleeps.."*

> *"Esa Einai el he'harim,*
>
> *me ayin yavo ez'ri?"*

"During times of war and distress Psalm 121 has been for many a source of comfort and healing help, she said. 'The Guardian of Israel neither slumbers nor sleeps.' How, then, we may ask, does a missile sent by evildoers ever reach its target? Why does illness ever prevail? Is not God somehow distant or in slumber when injustice occurs?

"According to Psalm 121, "The Guardian of Israel neither slumbers nor sleeps." What does it mean to be a guardian? A guardian watches and protects yet lets the young one run with the risk of falling. He sets boundaries for safety yet allows exploration. He does so because He knows that this is the only way the young one may learn and grow and one day help the world to be a better place.

"In a similar way during our time in the finite physical world, while we are not assured of a life without hardship in any way, we are assured of God's protection in an infinite way." The Psalm concludes:

"The Lord will guard you from all evil.

He will guard your soul.

The Lord will guard your going

and your coming

from now and for all time."

What does the Book of Psalms say about forgiveness?

Miriam slowly turned the page to Psalm 56:12

> *"In God I trust. I do not fear*
> *what can man do to me?"*

> *"B'Elokim batachti. Lo ira*
> *Ma ya'asei adam li."*

"It is much easier to speak about the distance between planets and the speed of light than to address the questions of human caused suffering.

"Why does brother harm brother? Why does an eager young man with the world before him fall and never reach 19? Why do people thoughtlessly hurt each other with words and deeds? Why?

Perhaps these questions are unanswerable. Therefore, it is left for us to give forgiveness, or if that is not possible then to release any hatred we may feel, and not to judge - to understand that God is the one true judge who knows the heart and mind of every person.

The 'Prayer Before Retiring at Night' contains a prayer of forgiveness:

"I hereby forgive anyone who angered or vexed me or sinned against me, either physically, or financially, against my honor or anything else that is mine; whether accidentally, intentionally, inadvertently or deliberately;
by speech or by deed,
in this incarnation or in any other.
May no man be punished on my account.
May it be Your will, Lord, my God
And God of my forefathers,
that I shall sin no more
nor repeat my sins,
neither shall I again anger You
nor do what is wrong in Your eyes.
The sins I have committed,
erase in Your abounding mercies,
but not through suffering or severe illnesses.

May the words of my mouth
and the meditation of my heart
be acceptable before You, Lord,
my Strength and my Redeemer."

(reprinted with kind permission from
Siddur Tehillat Hashem © 1995,.
Merkos L'inyonei Chinuch,
770 Eastern Parkway,
Brooklyn, New York.)

Miriam continued, "The psalmist asks: 'What can man do to me?'

"For each lifetime is but a moment relative to God's time. Once we realize and accept this, there is no fear of standing for what is right, for being brave and truthful and strong. Not to judge the why of the other but rather to persevere in our own mission in life: A life that is but a moment, and yet is integrally connected with the eternal."

What does the Book of Psalms say about dwelling in God's Presence?

Miriam opened her book to Psalm 61 and began:

"I will dwell in Your tent forever;

I will take refuge

in the shelter of your wings"

"What does it mean to dwell in God's tent - in the shelter of His wings? She asked.

"A tent shelters one from the burning sun and the raging storm yet allows the wanderer easy access to enter and exit at will. There are no doors, no gates, nothing is locked or barred. All is open for you and I to dwell in God's presence.

"With wings one can do the impossible, to see from afar, to rise above the hills, to be carried on air.

"Air, like the soul, can be neither seen nor touched; only its presence is felt.

Yet, light as air is, it can lift the heaviest C5 cargo jet carrying tanks across the oceans, skipping over mountains and never touching the ground.

"Like the tent, the wings give shelter from the elements; yet, the tent and wings are very different. The tent stands alone while wings work together as one. And so, perhaps Psalm 61 contains this important wisdom: it is together that we may truly fly."

What does the Book of Psalms say about unexplained things?

Miriam closed her eyes in quiet contemplation. With Psalm 119:18 before her she began:

"Unveil my eyes that I may behold

the wonders from Your Torah."

"Gal eyneni v'abiyta niflaos mi toraseycha."

"We know that the Torah was entrusted to us by God, and yet so much of the Torah is beyond our understanding. In the 18th passage of Psalm 119 - (18 meaning "chai" life), the psalmist pleas: "Uncover my eyes so that I may see the wonders of Your Torah..." The word "unveil" is "Gal" in Hebrew - the same letters as the word "Lag" – perhaps a reference to Lag BaOmer, she said.

"During the days between Passover and Shavuos, between the miracles of our release from the bondage of slavery and the receiving of the Torah (the waters of the infinite and our true birth as a free people in service of God) we celebrate the passing of a very special rabbi. Why do we celebrate this and why is there such a reference to plea for God to "unveil my eyes that I may behold the unexplained things of Your Torah."?

"It was 2,000 years ago, at the time of the first Lag BaOmer, and Israel had been conquered by the Roman Empire. It was a period of history in which the messianic era could have possibly begun. Two thousand years ago the factors were in place: Within Israel, there was a great military leader named Bar Kochba and great spiritual leaders like Rabbi Akiva who brought great holiness into the world. Throughout the empire there was widespread dissatisfaction with pagan rites and beliefs, and there were many people who were responsive to the Torah's message of love, hope and redemption.

"Tragically, it was not to be. The forces against the messianic era beginning before the suffering of the past twenty centuries were too great and the forces that would have helped bring it about fell short. Rome's military power and ability to bring its tremendous force down overwhelmed the small nation of Israel. All life was decimated, from the Temple which lay burned and leveled, to the population killed or enslaved. Even the trees were destroyed and the very name of the country was wiped away.

"However, it was not military might but spiritual failure which ensured that the messianic age was not to begin for at least another two thousand years. Spiritually, the Jews themselves fell short of the great spiritual and moral heights that were required. A plague ensued and all hopes for a messianic age were dashed.

"Then, in the midst of darkness, a new light emerged. Rabbi Shimon Bar Yochai revealed to a small group of students the mystical Zohar which uncovers the secrets which will eventually bring the coming of the messianic age. Thus, we commemorate Lag BaOmer as a day of revealed truths; in the hope, that each of us may help bring God's holiness into our corner of the world. For as the psalmist sings:

> *"Unveil my eyes that I may behold*
> *the wonders from Your Torah."*

What does the Book of Psalms say about fleeing?

Miriam turned the page to Psalm 11:

"I have placed my trust in the Lord;

Thus, how can you say of my soul,

Your mountain, that it flees like a bird?"

"For one who has taken refuge in God, this means one's soul is connected to its source. Although we do not always understand why events happen the way they do, the Holy One, Blessed is He, is the one refuge that transcends all time and all occurrences.

"It is written that the Messianic era can be brought forth in our time by these three things: "teshuva" - returning to closeness with God, "tzedaka" - giving charity and helping one another and "tefilla" - praying.

"When we are faced with challenges and we feel like fleeing like a bird, the refuge we seek is close at hand. It is as close as the person standing next to us as we help one another and pray for one another."

What does the Book of Psalms say about respectfulness and kindness?

Miriam opened to a particularly worn page containing Psalm 5:8 and she started to sing a joyous melody:

"And I, through the abundance

of your kindness,

will I enter Your house."

"Ve ani, berov chasdecha, avo beysecha."

She described: "He was called upon by the king to curse Israel. Famous for his abilities to channel the spiritual forces to his will, Bilam, had this simple task before him. It was not so simple, however.

"For as he stood gazing upon the tents of Israel, he found he was unable to articulate the words that would bring the dreaded curse down. His senses were overwhelmed with the awareness of the kindness and modesty of the Children of Israel. Their tents were arranged so that privacy would be respected. Their speech was not focused on the personal lives of their neighbors, rather they spoke of gratitude for God's blessings and they focused their lives on serving God with kindness and helpfulness.

"God then performed a miracle and caused his words to form the blessing that we now know as 'Ma Tovu' "How good".

"How goodly are your tents O' Jacob.
Your dwelling places Israel.
And I, through the abundance of
your kindness,
I will enter your house."

"Ma tovu ohalecha Yaakov
Mishkinotecha Israel.
V' ani b'rov chasdecha
Avo vetecha."

"For, it is the abundance of God's kindness that brings souls closer to Him. The kindness we sense when we think about

Sarah's tent: A tent glowing from the light of holiness that illuminated from one Shabbos to the next. A tent sheltered by spiritual clouds and challah that stayed fresh all week so that passersby would be nourished physically and spiritually.

"For the kindness of the Creator of the Universe is expressed by each of us every day in our lives. We may express God's kindness through consideration, by respecting the privacy of our neighbors and friends, through everyday conversation and action by focusing on holy words and thoughts, or through awareness of miracles such as the light, clouds and challah of Sarah's blessed tent.

"It is no coincidence that the 'Mishkan' (the tabernacle in the desert) and the 'Beis Ha Mikdash' (the Holy Temple in Jerusalem) were fashioned after Sarah's tent. Sarah's tent brings to mind our own home. Thus revealing that the holiest place on earth is as close as the place we dwell in each day. And as Bilam found by miracle and much to his surprise, this abundant kindness can turn a dreaded curse into beautiful blessing for all."

What does the Book of Psalms say about basic everyday life?

Miriam opened her book to the very beginning, Psalm 1.

"Fortunate is the man that has not walked

in the counsel of the wicked.

Nor stood in the path of the sinners,

nor sat in the company of scorners."

"Ashrei ha ish asher lo halach

ba atsat risha'eem,

u viderech chata'eem lo amad,

u vimoshav letsee lo yashav."

"Walking, standing and sitting refer to where we are and what we are doing, she explained. The very first psalm begins not with distant esoteric truths but with practical guidelines. Before I can begin my spiritual quest, before I can reach the heights of enlightenment, I must first learn to walk. Thus, Psalm 1 begins with the basics: how to walk, stand and sit through life.

"Yet, mundane and worldly as these concerns are: Who we take counsel from, which path we stand upon, which sessions are we immersed in, what we do each moment. As we gather these moments together they form a cohesive whole that becomes our life."

As the psalmist concludes:

"Rather his desire

is in the Torah of the Lord,

and in his Torah

he meditates day and night.

He shall be like a tree

planted by streams of water

That yields its fruit in its season

and whose leaf does not wither."

What does the Book of Psalms say about striving for peace in the midst of war?

Thoughts of Elisha, a young man who had been severely injured in battle, came to mind and the women thought of his gentle nature.

Miriam closed her eyes in thought and then began to recite Psalm 2:

"Why do nations gather

and peoples speak futility?

The kings of the earth stand up,

and rulers conspire together?"

"Lama ragshu goim

u l'umim yehgu-rik?

"The question of 'why do great nations conspire to do harm?' - has been with us for many generations. On outward

69

appearance, it seems as if the physical world of great nations and regimes is very powerful indeed. When the Roman army marched in unison with great armor and weapons, or when the Blitzkrieg blazed across the land, it was easy to take notice.

"And today, when entire regions of the world coordinate strategies aimed to destroy a tiny peaceful nation, when brutal atrocities are carried against innocents and the world sits silent. It is easy to feel that the forces of man are great and that we who strive for good have no chance against overwhelming odds.

"Although, it sometimes feels that all is lost, that the regimes who seek power over man have triumphed. The reality is the power of the Almighty is much greater."

As Psalm 2 concludes:

> *'Fortunate are all*
> *who put their trust in Him.'*

"Great nations conspiring to carry out their conquests may seem powerful but these outward appearances are ephemeral, indeed."

"Yet, the One who creates and sustains all; the infinite complex universe and each one of us; while beyond our comprehension, surely encompasses the realm of the infinite where our soul may truly sing."

What does the book of Psalms say about Hope in the midst of hopelessness?

Miriam turned the page to Psalm 3:2 and softly recited these words:

> *"Lord how numerous are my oppressors!*
>
> *Many rise up against me.*
>
> *Many say of my soul*
>
> *'There is no salvation for him*
>
> *from God ever*
>
> *But You, Lord, are a shield for me"*

"The psalm begins by describing a situation that David finds himself in: seemingly hopeless," Miriam relates. "Much like Israel, he is surrounded by enemies. Many say there is no hope for survival? Many say this because it is obvious to all who observe. How can David survive when surrounded by tormentors? How can Israel survive when it is surrounded on all sides by overwhelming numbers of enemies? How can I survive when my life becomes overwhelmed with troubles? When viewed from the perspective of the physical world alone, when we are in the midst of a sea of troubles it is true there is little if any hope.

"The psalmist then reveals that the physical world is not all that exists. There is a miraculous aspect to all that is. David, like each of us, is not facing trials alone. With God, anything is possible - even getting through and triumphing in a seemingly impossible situation.

'With my voice I call to the Lord

and He answers me'

(Psalm 3:5).

"The true reality is we are not facing our trials alone. We are the children of a loving and compassionate God. And even when the limited physical world appears to be overwhelming, it is only appearances after all. The blessing of God is upon us always."

What does the Book of Psalms say about thankfulness?

Miriam turned to Psalm 50:14 and sang:

"Offer God thanks;

and fulfill your vows

to the Most High."

"God desires bringing about a state of honesty, humility and thankfulness in our hearts," she said. "Even the very name of the Jewish people is derived from the same three-letter root as thankfulness (Hey, Vav and Dalet as in 'hodu' 'thank'). The word 'Jewish' ('Yehudim') translates as 'thankful ones.'

"There is a beautiful prayer called the "Modei Ani" prayer that is recited each morning upon awakening:

"I offer thanks to You,

living and eternal King,

for You have mercifully restored

my soul within me;

Your faithfulness is great."

"Modei Ani lifanecha

Melech chai vikayam

Shehechezarta bee nishmati

bechemla raba emunatecha

.

"While God desires thankfulness in our hearts, this gratitude is indeed a gift of kindness to each of us. Our life is all the more blessed when we are thankful each day."

What does the Book of Psalms say about living in such a way that pleases God?

Miriam opened her book to Psalm 15 and began to sing the words of this timeless question:

> *"Who may abide in Your Tent O Lord?*
>
> *Who may dwell*
>
> *on Your holy mountain?"*

"A tent offers protection from the elements yet one is still part of the world around him, she said. A mountain offers the strongest foundation yet it is a high point from which one may see from afar with wisdom and clarity.

"The question each of us has wondered: How can I live my life in such a way that is pleasing to God? Perhaps it is a way of being, a way of speaking, a way of doing kindness and truthfulness in the world."

"The psalmist continues:

"One who walks blamelessly,

Acts justly and speaks the truth in his heart

Who has no slander on his tongue,

who has done his fellow man no evil."

"Residing in God's tent and dwelling on His Holy Mountain does not mean residing in a holy shrine and meditating from within its walls. It does not mean dwelling among the enlightened, powerful and well positioned. It does not mean covering oneself with special clothing or being admired by other people.

"Perhaps it does mean, that to dwell in God's tent, each and every day we treat those around us truthfully and kindly. Or as Grandma Ida would say: it's nice to be a 'mench,' which is a Yiddish word for a 'person.'"

What does the Book of Psalms say about miracles?

Miriam opened her book to Psalm 106

> *"Praise the Lord for He is good,*
>
> *for His kindness is everlasting."*

"Is not every miracle a kindness made visible?"

"Amazingly, the electromagnetic radiation from all objects above the temperature of absolute zero, which is -273 degrees centigrade, surrounds us all the times. A radio receiver tuned to the frequency of a radio station receives the electro and the magnetic phase. The radio broadcast station modulates the transmission and the radio circuit separates it as sound is produced. Sound waves push air molecules and enter our ear through the small opening in our outer ear canal. The sound waves vibrate our tympanic membrane, which then vibrates three tiny bones which then vibrate the oval window of the inner ear. In the inner ear, the cochlea changes these sound vibrations into electro-chemical nerve impulses carried by the acoustic nerve to the temporal lobe which is located in the side of our brain. Our brain converts these electro-chemical impulses into the sounds we comprehend as meaningful words, music and sounds of nature.

"In a similar way the sun at 5000 degrees centigrade emits direct electro-magnetic radiation. The sunlight radiates in in all directions at the speed of light, 186,000 miles per second. We receive this light by the vibration of free electrons in the retina in the back of our eye as it enters through the precisely sized opening of the iris of our eye. The retina changes the light energy into electro-chemical neural impulses carried by the optic nerve to the occipital lobe which is located in the back of our brain. Our brain converts these electro-chemical impulses into comprehensible images we call vision.

"A true wonder is, God's kindness occurs so routinely we cease to call it a miracle!"

What does the Book of Psalms say about sleep?

Miriam gently turned to Psalm 4:9 and sang softly,

"In peace and in harmony

I will lie down and sleep,

For You, Lord, will make me

to dwell securely."

"What does it mean to sleep?" she asked as she rested her chin on her hand.

"According to the Kabbala, Sleep has been compared to the 2,000 year exile, since during sleep, as during the exile, we are not able to see Godliness in the world. Light is hidden from our eyes.

"According to recent scientific discoveries, the reticular activating system, in the brain, is responsible for the transition from sleep to wakefulness. Still, it remains a mystery: what sleep is and why we need to sleep.

"Insight may be derived from the prayer recited upon awakening, the "Modei Ani" prayer, which expresses thankfulness to God who has returned my soul to me. The soul during sleep has loosened its bonds with the body. It is free to dwell in higher realms."

"Sleep is miraculous. It was in a dream state that the ladder was revealed to Jacob. It was from a dream state that Ezekiel wrote of his visions. From a spiritual point of view, sleep is a time of connection to the Creator of the World.

"The first sentence in the Torah states "In the beginning, God *creates* the heavens and the earth." According to the Baal Shem Tov, this teaches that God creates the world continually, moment by moment. In this way we are enabled to dwell securely in the moment to moment creation of the miraculous world we live in.

"When we make the transition from what we see and hear with our physical senses to the mysterious state of sleep, as we 'fall into sleep' each evening, we are journeying beyond our understanding. Yet with the awareness that God hears and answers my prayers and continually creates the worlds for my body and my soul to dwell; there, as the psalm conveys, like a comfortable pillow "I will lie down and sleep in peace and in harmony."

What does the Book of Psalms say about kindness filling the earth?

Miriam opened her book to Psalm 119:64 and sang:

"Your kindness, O Lord,
fills the earth"

"Hasdecha, Hashem, malea ha aretz..."

"What does the meaning of 'malea' 'fills?
When God's kindness fills the earth, it means that there is not one speck of space that can be found absent of God.

"It means the world is not on autopilot. God fills it with kindness and love. When we are aware of this reality that where ever we journey through this life God is there truly filling every speck of life even during times of trouble. This realization that "Your kindness, God fills the earth" is truly life altering."

What does the Book of Psalms say about perception?

Miriam opened her book to Psalm 106:

"Praise the Lord for He is good.

His kindness is everlasting."

"Within the sub-atomic structure, solid mass makes up less than one percent of an atom's size, she explained. The distance between atoms within molecules is sometimes compared to light years between planets. This means that a solid object is mostly empty space.

"Light is invisible, but it is needed for our vision to function. When we 'see' an optical illusion or mirage, what we think we see is not even there.

"Color is our brain's interpretation of light waves between the frequency of approximately 390 to 700 nm as they bounce off objects and enter our eyes. The color we see is the portion of the light waves that is not absorbed by the object. Therefore, the object we see is actually every color except the color we are seeing.

"Light functions simultaneously as a wave and a particle which are two very different things. And the mere act of observing an object will affect the way we perceive it.

"The universe consists of subatomic particles flying at high speeds around and through us. Yet, this is different from our sensual perception of the world we experience. Thus, it can be stated that the physical world we perceive through our senses is not all there is.

"Just as there are atoms and light waves beyond our ordinary perception there is also the infinite world of loving kindness that God has built for us. This is perceived through our soul rather than our physical senses. And just as we must open our eyes in order to see the physical part of life we must open the gates to our souls to perceive the spiritual.

We may open the gates to our souls by setting aside time to pray, to think, to sing, to dance, to meditate on the meaning of the words that God has brought to us through our sages; to be God's hands on earth as we help each other along the way"

What does the Book of Psalms say about the heavens?

Miriam turned to Psalm 102:26

"In the beginning

You laid the foundations of the earth,

and the heavens

are the work of Your hands."

"As we look up to the heavens, we are awestruck by the realization that infinity and the universe are truly incomprehensible. Yet there had to be a creator of this wonder. Surely it was not by happenstance that the universe with phenomena that span from galaxies to neutrinos to the DNA, inside each cell, came to be.

"Einstein once said "God does not play dice with the universe." The likelihood of all this complexity arising by accident has been compared to the likelihood of a bottle of ink that accidentally spills and randomly forms the words of the Constitution.

"The vast awesomeness of the world and all that is in it, prove there is an author. When we are aware that "the work of Your hands are in the heavens," when we see the world as it is, we realize that there must be an 'intelligent designer' of this limitless miraculous complexity.

"Perhaps, then we may begin to discover our purpose on earth, in the understanding that God is the source of all blessings, great and small."

What does the Book of Psalms say about thankfulness in the midst of hardship?

Miriam opened her book to Psalm 30:12 and sang a song of healing and renewal:

"You have turned my mourning into dancing.

You have undone my sackcloth

and girded me with joy.

Therefore my soul shall sing to You,

and not be silent;

Lord, my God, I will praise You forever."

"Limaan yizamercha chavod

V' lo yidom Hashem,

Elochai l' odecha."

"Psalm 30 expresses sheer gratitude to God; for being alive, for healing, for raising my soul up. The fact that I am able to recite this Psalm and sing to God is cause for infinite thankfulness.

"It is also recited during the holiday of Hanukah commemorating the rekindling of the Menorah in the Temple in Jerusalem. For the ancient Israelites, the Greek/Assyrian Empire had conquered the land they lived in, dictated the society's values, even taken over the Temple itself, the very spot of the Holy of Holies, the special place where God's presence rests on earth.

"Yet it was only temporary as times and conditions eventually changed. But throughout this and other difficult journeys, our soul's song of healing and renewal has long remained."

As Psalm 30 continues:

> *"Therefore my soul shall sing to You,*
>
> *and not be silent;*
>
> *Lord, my God,*
>
> *I will praise You forever."*

What does the Book of Psalms say about tests?

Miriam turned to Psalm 26:1

"By David, Judge me, O Lord,

for in my innocence I have walked,

And in the Lord I have trusted

I shall not falter.

Try me, Lord, and test me;

refine my mind and heart."

"Psalm 26 begins with a simple request for a test," Miriam explained. "David has experienced a special closeness to God. He has come very far in his life of devotion. Like a person who has just performed an amazing feat of jumping up high or doing a flip, he asks with excitement: 'Look at me! How am I doing?'

"As David learns, we are all human and with great limitations. When we think we are doing so well that we can ask for a test that is the time we get into trouble."

"David says *"Judge me God, for 'in my innocence I have walked.'"* This was the same expression that was used when Abraham was tested in his 10th and most difficult test. Possibly David was striving to reach the level of Abraham but, when he asked to be tested, God gave him the test of Bathsheba and that was a test David could not pass.

"God will give us tests during our life, to be sure. Some we will pass, some we will fail. The tests we are given will be in accordance with God's wisdom about what each of us needs to experience in this life and what we can handle. When we judge one another, we are really doing God's job and not ours. He is the true judge who knows what is in each of our hearts.

"Woven within the words of this psalm is a wisdom: Regardless of where we are at the moment, whether, as lofty as a brave King, who has dedicated his life to serving God and humanity, or as an ordinary person like me who may be afraid of a small bug - there is the concept of Trust, ('Bitachon' in Hebrew), trust in God's wisdom to give each of us the tests that we need in this lifetime."

"Although we may wish the tests were easier, as David learned, it is not a good idea to ask for more tests. Rather, simply to trust in God's wisdom and love and to continue as best we can, to walk a path of goodness in the world."

"David concludes with this realization:

"My foot stands on level ground;

In assemblies I will bless the Lord."

What does the Book of Psalms say about the right way to praise God?

Miriam sang the song of Psalm 150; A melody she carried oftentimes in her heart.

"Praise Him with the call of the shofar;

Praise Him with harp and lyre.

Praise Him with timbrel and dance;"

"... Let every soul Praise the Lord."

Her thoughts waxed poetic:

"The shofar: Open to God's holiness,
increasing from below to above.
The harp: Resonating together,
in harmony with God's love.

94

"The final psalm of the Book of Psalms sings of the many ways to praise God. Perhaps this teaches us that just as there are different instruments there are different ways each of us can serve God in holiness - different people, different ways of worship. All are loved by God.

"Additionally, the order itself reveals more and more involvement in the physical as the list goes on. The ways of worship go from the air (shofar) to the hands (lyre and harp) to the entire body (timbrel and dance). Perhaps this teaches that we may praise God by our spiritual openness - as well as our involvement in the physical world.

"There is also the aspect of this prayer that tells us that all are needed in the world. We can't possibly do it all by ourselves, all alone. We can't praise God by blowing a shofar, playing a lyre and a harp, drumming and dancing all at the same time. We need each other."

"Still one more way to think about this psalm is as a group. Just as the individual may praise God in varying ways, groups of people may serve Him in ways that are distinct, yet all are beloved by God."

What does the Book of Psalms say about troubles beyond our understanding?

Miriam opened her book to Psalm 74 and softy began:

"A maskil by Asaph.

Why, O God have you abandoned us forever,

Does Your wrath fume

against the sheep of Your pasture?

"Lama, Elokim, zanachta laneitsach?"

"A maskil is a psalm with a message so delicate that King David asks a special wise person to recite and interpret the words so that people may understand it better, according to Rashi. The word "maskil" shares the same 3-letter root as "sechel" or wisdom and understanding.

"A maskil is a musical instrument with a special capacity to enlighten the mind and inspire the heart, according to Meiri."

"Asking God the heartfelt question: 'Why have You abandoned us?' requires a special wisdom and understanding.

As Asaph laments:

"Remember Your congregation

which You acquired long ago,

the tribe of Your inheritance

whom You redeemed

and brought to Mount Zion,

where You rested Your Presence."

"Asaph concludes with a plea for God to remember what has happened to His people, to forget not the voice of oppression.

"Why does the psalmist implore God to remember? Surely, the Creator of the World could not be short of memory. God knows all that has happened and all that is in our heart. He remembers our struggles and our agonies. He knows the beautiful dawn that will follow the darkness of night."

"Thus, this maskil for Asaf the Seer expresses a clear acknowledgment: While a brighter future awaits and we understand that God has not forgotten us. Psalm 74 reminds us that sometimes God sends a wise instrument of understanding to help us when there are troubles beyond our comprehension. Other times, we may be the maskil who offers help to another person who needs an extra lift to survive." Psalm 74 conveys that there are times when we need one other to help us through the great challenges of our life."

What does the Book of Psalms say? Does God answer my prayers?

Miriam opened her Book to Psalm 20, a psalm of healing.

"May the Lord answer you

on the day of distress.

May the name of the God of Jacob

fortify you.

May He send your help

from the Sanctuary,

and support you from Zion."

"In Hebrew the phrase 'May God answer you' can be translated as: 'a'anancha,' 'You answer, God' - this reveals that it can be read as a statement of something that presently is. For it is as if we have called, He has answered. He is just waiting for us to hear it. There is no waiting. He has already answered our prayers."

"The Psalm states that the Sanctuary will be where the help will be dispatched from and Zion as the place from where the support will come.

"The Sanctuary refers to the Holy of Holies inside the Temple in Jerusalem, according to classic sources. This is the special place where God's divine presence rests. Our help will be dispatched from the holiest place in the world.

"If each of us can be likened to the Temple in Jerusalem, there too is a special place within us that God's divine presence dwells, a spark of holiness. We can know that God's answers to our prayers of help are not some far away abstract concept. They are close at hand and already here."

What do Psalms say about questions that I have for God?

Miriam opened her book to psalm 27:4 and sang a beautiful melody. The page, worn and tattered, but whose words were clear:

"One thing I have asked of the Lord,

this I seek:

that I may dwell in the House of the Lord

all the days of my life,

to behold the pleasantness of the Lord

and to meditate in His Sanctuary."

She wondered: "What would I ask of the Creator of the World if I had the chance to ask not one question but as many as I wished?

"Why and how was the universe created? What are the true laws of all of physics? How can we cure all disease? Why is there so much suffering on earth? How can we bring peace and tranquility to all? If I were to ask questions I would have a lot to ask.

"Then, finally, after all my questions were answered, all my curiosity satisfied, all the endless hours of questions and answers completed - the essence would then be - as David so insightfully prayed

"...that shall I seek to dwell

in the House of the Lord

all the days of my life,

to behold the pleasantness of the Lord

and to meditate in His Sanctuary..."

What does the Book of Psalms say in my time of need?

Miriam opened her book to Psalm 23: The tear-stains on the page reminders of her loss.

"The Lord is my shepherd

I shall lack nothing

He lays me down in green pastures.

He leads me beside still waters.

He revives my soul.

He directs me in paths of righteousness

for the sake of His name.

Though I walk in the valley

of the shadow of death

I will fear no evil

For You are with me."

"What does it mean to be a shepherd?" she asked.

"A shepherd watches over each sheep. And when one wanders off and loses his way, the shepherd rescues him. He may have strayed inches from a cliff, high up on a steep slippery embankment. Nevertheless, the shepherd finds a way to rescue him even in the most dangerous circumstances. The shepherd rescues him without recrimination only with understanding and compassion.

"On the side of the mountain, as the sheep balances by the crest of a rocky cliff, looking down at the rocks far below, there is great fear.

"Down in the valley, where predators can see him from far away, as the sheep passes, sensing the danger all around him, there is great fear.

"Once aware that the shepherd is close by, whether the sheep is resting in a peaceful lush meadow or passing through a valley surrounded by those who strive to do him harm, there is no fear. He knows he is protected.

"In a similar way, in our lifetime, whether we are enjoying a peaceful day or enduring a dangerous journey of struggle and loss, God is with us through each moment, each step of the way.

"And throughout this journey that is our life, as David sings …

"You have anointed my head with oil;

My cup is full.

May only goodness and kindness

pursue me all the days of my life,

and I will dwell in the house of the Lord

for the length of days."

"Ach tov v'chesed

Yir'd'funi kal Y'mai chayai

V'shv'ti b'veit Hashem l'orech yamim."

What does the Book of Psalms say about service?

Miriam eyes smiled as she turned to Psalm 100

.

"A Psalm of Thanksgiving.

Let all the earth sing in jubilation to the Lord.

Serve the Lord with joy;

come before Him with exultation."

She described a scene from Temple times long ago:

"The children skipped joyfully ahead of the adults, careful not to drop the warm bread they each carried in their hands. The smoothly polished white marble of the Temple reflected the gentle sunlight as the harmonies of the Levite choirs resounded throughout the courtyard. As the loaves of bread were gently placed upon the table, and the music of psalms softly filled the air, it felt as if one's soul had already taken flight.

"The Thanksgiving offering of bread accompanied by Psalm 100, was made during the time of the Temple in Jerusalem. It is the only offering which will still be made during the Messianic era. For even when the world is in a highly refined spiritual state, and there is peace on earth, we will need to give thanks to God for His many blessings. It is also a psalm for all people everywhere, and for all time.

"Psalm 100, the Psalm of Thanksgiving, is recited daily in the Jewish prayer book. According to the Siddur She'lah and Ya'avits, each and every day people experience miracles whether or not they realize it.

"However, Psalm 100, the Psalm of Thanks, begins with words of service."

"A Psalm of Thanksgiving.

Let all the earth sing

in jubilation to the Lord.

Serve the Lord with joy..."

"What does it mean to serve God with joy?"

107

"The word "serve" or "ivdu" is derived from the same root as the word for "slave" or "eved" in Hebrew. Service is not easy. As we go about our daily lives, the reality is we are all servants. This applies even to a president or king. No matter where in life we find ourselves, whether high or low on the social strata, somehow we are each serving someone or something most of the time. Yet, the psalmist sings: "Serve God with joy…""

"When we are immersed in thoughts, speech or action, that as a result, cause us to forget about God, it is an indication that we are putting something above God; for truly there is cause to be grateful for His blessings each moment we are alive.

"How do we serve God with joy?"

"One way we serve God with joy is by serving others each day. It is almost as if there is a special "barometer" of joy inside each of us. When we go out of our way to help someone; when we pray for someone; when we study the words of the Torah; our joy increases. The very act of serving God brings an inner sense of joy.

"In modern times, we don't bring three loaves of bread to the Temple as the Levite choirs sing the Psalm of Thanksgiving. "

"Instead we bring the bread of our efforts. We bring service with joy.

"And as we serve God with joy, this feeling of joy that we experience deep inside has a multiplying effect, much like the pebble that creates waves as it touches the water.
The goodness and kindness grows and multiplies as each person continues to add to this cycle of service and gratitude to the One who created the world."

What does the Book of Psalms say about the Redemption?

Miriam read from Psalm 99:1

"When God will reveal His kingship,

the nations will tremble;

The earth will quake upon Him

who is enthroned upon the cherubim."

She explained: "Moses wrote this psalm in foreknowledge of a time just before the redemption. It mentions the world shaking in awe before God who is enthroned upon the Cherubim ("Keruvim" in Hebrew).

"So what are Keruvim?"

"We read about them in Exodus, as the Children of Israel, a population of more than a million souls, dwells in the desert. Their very life is sustained by miracle. They eat Manna which falls from heaven each morning. The water they drink springs forth miraculously. They do not know whether they will camp for a day or a year but they follow God's miraculous guidance each and every day.

"Then God gives special directions about building a Mishkan, or Sanctuary, in the desert. As part of the directions, God instructs the Children of Israel to hammer out, from a single piece of gold, two Cherubim as part of a cover for the Ark which will protect the Ten Commandments. Cherubim were also embroidered on the curtains that formed the ceiling of the Sanctuary in which Hashem's presence dwelled. Ezekiel, in his dream, (Ezekiel 10) saw above the Cherubim something like a sapphire stone the appearance of a throne. (The Ten Commandments and the staff of Moses, on which the 12 tribes of Israel were engraved, were both made of sapphire stone.)

"Great sages throughout the centuries have explained the meaning of the Cherubim. They have come to signify the pure love of a child, brotherly love, male and female love, and the love of the people of Israel, among other descriptions. They are also guardians on the pathway to the Tree of Knowledge so that Adam and Eve do not return to the Garden of Eden. They carry swords of fire that swing back and forth blocking the way. This could also be a statement of love as a guardian or protector.

"The Cherubim have many forms and attributes. Perhaps we can better understand them by seeing where God placed them and what task He gave them. For, like all beings created by God, they are serving Him in some way.

"We know that the Cherubim guarded the Garden of Eden, the Sanctuary in the desert and the Tablets of the Ten Commandments.

"The Garden of Eden marks the transition of mankind from a supernal to an earthy existence. The Sanctuary in the desert marks the transition of the Children of Israel from slaves to a free nation guided to the Holy Land by God's presence. The Ten Commandments marks the transition from a world where cruelty was commonplace and acceptable to a world where peace, justice and Godliness are possible. In Psalm 99, Moses describes the Cherubim as an integral part of the redemption of mankind, which marks the transition to a world where war and disease will no longer exist."

"In all these examples, the Cherubim are protecting something very important to God and that protection has something to do with love.

"Whether it is the Garden of Eden, the Sanctuary, the Ten Commandments, or the time when God's kingship will reign; the power of love was chosen by God to protect His most precious gifts to mankind.

"Is it possible that the love is more important than we imagine?"

What does the Book of Psalms say about blessing?

Miriam paused and turned to Psalm 67

"May God be gracious to us
and bless us;
May He make His countenance shine upon us
forever,"

"Elokim y'hanenu.
viy varcheynu ya er panav itanu selah."

"This psalms brings to mind a very special blessing," written by God himself. He spoke to Moses and told him to teach these words to Aaron and his sons so they shall know how to bless the Children of Israel.

"As we part ways and as you continue to write the amazing book that is your life on earth – exploring adventures of learning, laughter and love – courage, generosity and gratitude, I wish to impart this blessing to you."

"And Miriam began to sing a timeless melody of the heavenly spheres infused with love and hope in her heart:

"May God bless you and guard you

May God shine His countenance upon you

and have mercy upon you.

May God give favor to you

and give you peace. "

Then God says:

"And they will place My name

upon the children of Israel

And I will bless them. "

Y'varech'cha Hashem v'yish'mirecha.

Ya'er Hashem panaiv eleicha

V'yichugecha

yisa Hashem panaiv eleicha

v'yasem lecha shalom

About the author
and how this book came to be

As a child I remember those moments walking with my mother and sitting next to her as we read psalms together. As a teenager, I heard that a local synagogue needed someone to help play guitar for the congregation. I noticed that the songs were based on the words of psalms in the original Hebrew.

The positive impact of psalms became apparent when I lived in Israel in 1981. There was an orphanage where I volunteered each week, and was often asked to play music. The children derived great comfort from the psalms. I played and sang psalms at the Machon Alte Jewish School in Tsefat, at the International Festival at Haifa University and the Jerusalem Festival in Jerusalem. In Israel, people often sang along, and I saw on the faces of those who knew the words much better than I, just how meaningful and inspiring the psalms were.

Years later, while living in Fort Benning Army post, as a military wife, I was honored to give a class for Jewish soldiers on Sunday mornings. We discussed the Torah portion and my children and I sang psalms with the soldiers. I also served as Music Director for the Columbus Jewish Religious School where I taught the children songs from the Book of Psalms.

I became aware of the need for increased awareness of psalms one evening while listening to a radio show. The subject was "Psalms", and the listeners were told they would hear a performance of psalms in Hebrew. I was surprised to hear psalms performed so that each syllable was the same as the syllable before it. The meaning, passion, and heartfelt expression were missing. I felt that perhaps people were not aware of how beautiful and helpful psalms could be.

Soon after, I played the instruments and recorded the beautiful voices of my children singing psalms. I gave these CDs to family and friends, especially if there was someone in need of strength and inspiration.

I was able to enjoy sharing this music with my dear mother (of blessed memory). She was the kind of person who, when she walked into a room, she filled it with love, goodness and a special joy of life. Even when she was ill, the nurses would take their breaks in her room so they could seek her advice. She usually recommended enjoying each moment and not forgetting to dance.

Eight months after she passed away, I experienced a sudden loss of both speech and comprehension. The CT performed in the emergency room revealed that a 5 cm mass had caused my brain to move all the way across the midline and had blocked a part of my brain that carries the cerebrospinal fluid. It was only a matter of time before pressure could build up and cause instant death. I was airlifted by helicopter and later diagnosed with a benign High Grade Meningioma.

After the surgery to remove the tumor, I experienced something amazing. As my husband and children recited psalms for me, I was so grateful and I could feel the healing and strength. I was thankful and amazed to learn that a whole community gathered to recite tehillim for me.

As I thought of the melodies and words of psalms, especially Lev Tahor (Psalm 51), Gam Ki Elech (Psalm 23) and Keli Ata (Psalm 119), it felt as if the un-wellness that I was experiencing was instantly dissolved.

I discovered many years later an explanation of what I had experienced. It seems the most frequent Hebrew word that is written to describe the psalm as it first begins is "mizmor." Mizmor has the same root as the word "zamar" – "to make music" and "zamair" which means to "cut off" or "prune."

According to Rabbi Nachman of Breslov, psalms are very effective in "cutting off" negative spiritual forces, which are symbolized as briars and thorns. (according to "Jewish Spiritual Practices" by Yitzhak Buxbaum).

Coming so close to dying, I reflected upon what had just transpired. I felt an overwhelming sense of gratitude to God to be alive and to be given a second chance at life and certain concepts became very clear:

- Life is a complex symphony of miracles. Many psalms begin: "For the Conductor". God is the conductor, the composer, the instruments, and much more. The synchronicity that needed to occur so that I would be exactly where I am today is truly miraculous. As it is for each of us.

- God is the only One who truly understands the heart, mind and soul of every person. It is not for us to judge one another, only to do what is right and good.

- Each moment is very precious.

My time on earth is limited to a certain number of moments. If
this were my last hour, I would do something meaningful.
This day and this hour are also precious.

And so was born this project to spread psalms in honor of Sally
Fuchs, Tsipora bas Yosef and Yitka (of blessed memory) and
Morris Mizrachi, Moshe ben Chaim Eliezer and Miriam Faigey
(of blessed memory). They taught us love, laughter, kindness
and joyful appreciation for Hashem's everyday gifts.

Free Download Information

This book comes with free downloadable content which can be found at:

www.cdbaby.com/artist/taramizrachi

1. Under the heading "Music" click on the title of the album "Psalms for Everyone"
2. Click "Download $0.00" and
3. Click "Check Out" and follow prompts.

These downloads are offered in the hope they will enhance the reader's experience of psalms, as Psalms were originally composed and expressed in the form of song,

The musical renditions of psalms bring to mind a time in ancient Israel as people camped for the night along walking paths on their journey to Jerusalem, singing and dancing together with joy. These scenes have reoccurred throughout history: whether in the shtetls of Eastern Europe, the mellahs of Morocco, the suburbs of America, or the border towns of Southern Israel. As people gather together to sing the psalms of their ancestors, each person, and the world as a whole, experiences an increase in strength and holiness in amazing and miraculous ways. And so we are brought full circle to the words of a great sage of long ago:

"Know that the chapters of Psalms break through all barriers and soar aloft from level to level unimpeded. They intercede before the Master of the Universe and secure their effect with kindness and mercy."

- "The Tzemach Tzedek",
3rd Lubavitcher Rebbe, (1789-1866)

Glossary/Contents

Why Recite the Psalms?

Kotel: The Western Wall surrounding the Temple in Jerusalem which was built by King Solomon in 832 BCE.

Shimon Bar Yochai: A sage who was a disciple of Rabbi Akiva during the latter part of the First Century. After the death of Rabbi Akiva, he was forced to go into hiding and he lived in a cave for 14 years during which time he wrote the mystical works of the Kabbalah.

Tzefat: Safed - City in the Galilea region of Northern Israel where Rabbi Shimon bar Yochai and his son lived. Their grave site is nearby in Meron.

A Solitary Flame

Calanit flower: A flower with 5-8 petals of red, white, blue or violet, the Calanit flower has been named the National Flower of Israel and grows wildly throughout the area. It is also known as Anemone Coronaria.

King David: King of Israel who wrote most of the psalms. King David ruled Israel from 1010-970 BCE, approximately 3000 years ago.

Levite Choirs: musicians and professional liturgical singers who led the congregation of Israel in prayer during Temple times. (I Chron 15:16, 25:6–7

Mikvah: a ritual bath which brings purification. It signifies the transition from a lower to a higher spiritual state. Rabbi Aryeh Kaplan, in "Waters of Eden" made a comparison to the the waters that flowed out of the Garden of Eden in which Adam and Eve immersed themselves in after bringing death into the world.

Passover: Holiday which commemorates God liberating the Children of Israel from slavery in Egypt.

Shabbas: The Sabbath day, also called "Shabbat" in Hebrew. It is listed in the Ten Commandments as a day to remember and make holy. In the Jewish calendar it falls from Friday sunset to Saturday sunset.

Shavuot: Holiday which commemorates the receiving of the Ten Commandments at Mount Sinai. **Shir Ha'maalot: Songs of Ascent**: Fifteen Psalms 120-134 that were written by King David. They were sung by worshipper as they ascended on their way to Jerusalem during the three major festival and as they ascended the steps of the Temple.

Tehillim: "Psalms" meaning "Praises" in Hebrew.

Temple: The Temple in Jerusalem which was built by King Solomon by 832 BCE. It is called the Beis Hamikdash in Hebrew and housed the Holy of Holies.

Three Festivals: Passover, Shavuot and Sukkot – During the three major festivals, pilgrims walked for many miles to participate in prayers at the Temple in Jerusalem. **Passover:** commemorates God liberating the Children of Israel from slavery in Egypt, **Shavuot:** commemorates the receiving of the Ten Commandments at Mount Sinai; and **Sukkot:** commemorates the wandering of the Children of Israel through the desert as God led them by clouds of glory. People built temporary dwellings or Sukkot to dwell in.

Torah: The Five Books of Moses: Genesis, Exodus, Leviticus, Numbers, Deuteronomy. The Torah in a general sense can also refer to the entire Bible, the commentaries, the parables and the entire Talmud.

Psalm 34:13 – Living Each Day

Psalm 118:19 – Prayer
> **Tzedek:** Righteousness or Saintliness

Psalm 89:3 – Kindness

Psalm 31:4 – Protection

Psalm 19 – Speech

Psalm 65 – Silence

Psalm 52:10 – Trust

Psalm 72 – Wisdom

Psalm 22:2 – Faith during Hardship:
> **Persian Empire:** The Persian Empire was based around what is today modern day Iran. The Persian Empire spanned throughout the Middle East beginning in 550 BCE, interrupted by the Muslim conquest in 651 AD and later conquered by the Mongol conquest in 1218 CE. The religion of the Persian Empire was Zoroastrianism.

Psalm 75 – Success

Psalm 84:2 – God's Dwelling Places
> **Hashem:** God's name which is impossible to pronounce. "Hashem" in Hebrew means "The Name" (of God). In the Bible it is written in 4 letters, which are often mispronounced. These 4 letters share the same Hebrew root as "to be." "I am that I am" is an excellent translation in terms the meaning. The word "Hashem" is used in

ordinary conversation out of respect for the 2nd Commandment which says not to take God's name in vain.

Psalm 19:8 – The Torah

Shavuot: A holiday commemorating the day the Ten Commandments were received at Mount Sinai. Traditionally the 49 days from Passover until Shavuot are counted and Shavuot is celebrated with dairy foods and studying of the Torah, especially the Book of Ruth and the Ten Commandments.

Sons of Korah: Korah joined a revolt against Moses' leadership and along with his cohorts, he was consumed by the earth (Numbers 26:11). His young sons were spared. They worked caring for the Tabernacle and generations later some of them fought beside David and became notable warriors. During King David's time the descendants of Korah were notable for their leadership and talent in the orchestra and choir. Heman, Asaph and Ethan were beautiful singers and composers. About 25 of the psalms are attributed to the Sons of Korah including, Psalm 42-50, 62 and 72-85, including Psalm 84, "How lovely is your dwelling place, O God."

Psalm 121 – Protection

Psalm 56:12 – Forgiveness

Psalm 61 – Dwelling in God's Presence

Psalm 119:8 – Unexplained Things

Bar Kokhba: Shimon Bar Kokhba was a descendant of the Davidic line who led Israel in a revolt against the

Roman rule. He died in a massive battle at Bethar in the Judean Hills in 134 CE.

Chai: - "Life." (in Hebrew)

Gal: - "Uncover" (in Hebrew)

Lag B'Omer: A holiday which falls between Passover and Shavuot and marks the ending of a plague during the time of Rabbi Akiva who lived during the first century. It also marks the anniversary of the passing of Rabbi Shimon Bar Yochai.

Shimon Bar Yochai: A sage who was a disciple of Rabbi Akiva who lived during the destruction of the Temple in Jerusalem in 70 CE. According to legend he lived in a cave for 14 years during which time he wrote the mystical works of the Kabbalah.

Rabbi Akiva: A sage and leading contributor of many scholarly works, including the mishna and the Talmud. He lived during the latter part of the first century at the time the Romans had conquered Israel. He began his studies at the age of 40 and is known for his humility and wisdom and great faith and courage.

Roman Empire: An empire which began in 27 BCE. It lasted until 395 CE in Europe and 1453 CE in the Middle East. At its height in 98 CE, the Roman Empire included an area of 5 million square kilometers and possibly as many as 100 million people. In modern terms, this would include 40 countries.

Psalm 11 – Fleeing

The Holy One Blessed Is He: A reference to God. In Hebrew it is pronounced "Ha Kadosh Baruchu."

Teshuva: Repentance – In Hebrew the literal translation is "returning" (to God).

Tzedakah: Charity - The word is derived from the Hebrew root meaning righteousness, justice and fairness.

Tefilah: Prayer – The word is derived from the Hebrew root meaning "to judge   oneself" referring to the quiet introspection that prayer provides as we increase our awareness of God.

21 Psalm 5:8 – Respectfulness

Beis Hamikdash: The magnificent Temple built by King Solomon in 967 BCE (Deuteronomy 12:2) (nearly 3000 years ago). The Beis Hamikdash or Temple was the site of worship where the people of Israel journeyed during the three major festivals and it was the site of the Holy of Holies in which the Ten Commandments rested. Daily prayers and offerings were made there, well trained musicians and Levite choirs sang Psalms of Praise. It was sacked by the King of Assyria in 700 BCE and destroyed by the Babylonians in 586 BCE. It was rebuilt in 515 BCE (Book of Ezra) and later destroyed by the Romans in 70 CE. Jewish people have been worshiping at the Western Wall of the Temple ever since then and to this very day.

Bilaam: A diviner who was called upon by King Balak to curse Israel. He was unable to do so as God had miraculously prevented him from forming the words. (Numbers 22)

Challah: A special bread which is braided. It is eaten on Shabbas and holidays. Before baking, a portion is separated and a blessing is recited.

Mishkan: Tabernacle – The temporary dwelling place of God's presence in the desert. (Exodus 25). It housed the Holy of Holies. The Mishkan shares the same Hebrew root as the word "Shechina" meaning "God's presence." The Children of Israel carried it and set it up wherever they dwelled during their forty years of wandering the desert.

Sarah: Wife of Abraham. She welcomed guests and was known for her beauty, kindness and sense of humor. She named her son Isaac which means "laughter" in Hebrew.

Shabbas: The Sabbath day, also called "Shabbat" in Hebrew. It is listed in the Ten Commandments as a day to remember and make holy. In the Jewish calendar it occurs from Friday sunset to Saturday sunset.

Psalm 1 – Everyday Life

Torah: The Five Books of Moses: Genesis, Exodus, Leviticus, Numbers, Deuteronomy. The Torah in a general sense can also refer to the entire Bible, the commentaries, the parables and the entire Talmud.

Psalm 2 – Peace

Psalm 3:2 – Hope

Psalm 50:14 – Thankfulness

Hodu: Give Thanks - (in Hebrew). Hodu shares the same Hebrew root as the word "Toda" "thank" and "Yehudim" "Jews."

Psalm 15 – Living Each Day

Mentsh: Human Being/Person (in Yiddish). It refers to a person of good character.

Psalm 106 – Miracles

Psalm 4 – Sleep

Jacob's ladder: Jacob dreamed of a ladder in which angels were ascending and descending between earth and heaven (Genesis 28:10).
Ezekiel's dream: (Ezekiel 1:1-28)
Baal Shem Tov: A Jewish mystical rabbi and founder of the Hasidic movement whose name translates as "Master of the Good Name." He is known to have performed miracles and he taught about the immense importance of love for one another and love for God. He lived from approximately 1700-1760.

Psalm 119 – Kindness on Earth

Psalm 106 – Perception

Psalm 102:26 – The Heavens

Psalm 30 – Thankfulness

Chanukah: A holiday celebrating the rededication of the Temple in Jerusalem and the miracle of the light of the menorah which lasted eight days. Although there was only enough oil for one day, the oil lasted eight days thereby allowing time for the Israelites to purify new oil for the Temple.
Greek/Syrian Empire: A great Hellenistic empire founded by Seleucus , expanded by Alexander the Great and ruled by his descendants roughly from 312 BCE-63

BCE. It spanned from Greece through Persia (Iran). After a military revolt in 143 BCE, the Israelites, led by Judah Maccabee and his sons, were able to reestablish sovereignty over the Temple in Jerusalem.

Psalm 26 – Life's Tests

Abraham's 10th test: The Binding of Isaac - (Genesis 22:2)

Bathsheva: The wife of David and the mother of Solomon. (2 Samuel 11-12). She was first seen by David as she bathed on a rooftop.

Psalm 150 – How to Praise God

Lyre: Stringed instrument primarily played as chords to accompany the choir in Jerusalem. It had a sound box for resonance and its name "kinor" in Hebrew resembles the word "kineret" or the Sea of Galiliea. Some suggest this may reference its shape.

Nevel: Harp

Timbrel: Tamborine

Shofar: A wind instrument formed from a ram's horn. Torah commentators have described it as resembling the sound of a cry. It has been sounded at Mount Sinai (Exodus 19:16), as a battle cry (Josh. 6:4' Judges 3:27, 7:16, 20; I Sam. 8:3), in the Levite Choirs during Temple times, and during special days of the Jewish calendar (for example: the Jubilee year, the month of Elul, Rosh Hashanah and Yom Kippur.)

Psalm 74 – Troubles Beyond Our Understanding

Psalm 20 – Answers – Does God Hear My Prayers?

Zion: Jerusalem, Israel - It refers also to Mount Zion near Jerusalem (2 Samuel 5:7). In Kabbalah it refers to the spiritual point where reality comes forth. It is centered in the Holy of Holies in the Temple in Jerusalem.

Psalm 27 – Questions I Have For God

Psalm 23 – My Time of Need

Psalm 100 – Service

Levite Choirs – The musicians and liturgical singers who led the congregation of Israel in prayer during the time of the Temple in Jerusalem from 967-586 BCE and from 515 BCE-70 CE. Four thousand singers were appointed, according to a census at the time of King David. (I Chron. 15:16, 25:6–7).

Psalm 99 – Redemption

Mishkan: Tabernacle – The temporary dwelling place of God's presence in the desert. (Exodus 25). It housed the Holy of Holies. The Mishkan shares the same Hebrew root as the word "Shechina" meaning God's presence. The Children of Israel carried the Mishkah and set it up where they camped.

Psalm 67 – A Blessing

About the Author

Mizmor: a melody.

Rabbi Nachman of Breslov: (1772-1810) Great-grandson of the Baal Shem Tov. He combined great scholarship with mystical concepts. He taught people to find a special closeness with God and to speak with God as one would speak with a dearest friend.

Zamar: to make music

Zamair: to prune or trim

Notes

"SOFTWARE FOR THE SOUL – PSALMS FOR EVERYONE, DISCOVERING THE INNER MEANINGS" is available at local book stores, local libraries, Mayo Clinic Library, academic institutions, Amazon.com, Amazon Europe, Create Space e-store and other major book outlets.

Digital books are available through Kindle.com and BarnesandNoble.com.

Audio books are available through Amazon.com, itunes.com, and Audible.com.

Wholesale copies are available through third party distributors: Ingram, and Baker & Taylor respectively.

If you would like to make this book available to your organization at reduced rates or to book speaking engagements contact: taramizrachi@gmail.com.

For more articles and music based on Psalms visit www.psalmsonline.org or www.psalms-tehillim.com.

Made in the USA
Middletown, DE
03 February 2023

23834367R00076